My Lord God,

I have no idea where I am going.

I do not see the road ahead of me.

I cannot know for certain where it will end.

Nor do I really know myself,

and the fact that I think I am following your will

does not mean that I am actually doing so.

But I believe that the desire to please you

does in fact please you.

And I hope I have that desire

in all that I am doing.

I hope that I will never do anything

apart from that desire.

And I know that if I do this you will

lead me by the right road,

though I may know nothing about it.

Therefore will I trust you always though

I may seem to be lost and in the shadow of death.

I will not fear, for you are ever with me,

and you will never leave me to face my perils alone.

Thomas Merton

Jesus replied, "Love the Lord your God with all your heart and with all your soul and with all your mind.' This is the first and greatest commandment. And the second is like it: 'Love your neighbor as yourself.'
Matthew 22:37-40

The essence of the Christian life is a **tri-dimensional relational movement**; toward **God**, **others** and **ourselves**. But it's incredibly hard to love what we do not know.

KNOW THYSELF

"How can you draw close to God when you are far from your own self?"
Saint Augustine

"Without knowledge of self, there is no knowledge of God. Our wisdom, insofar as it ought to be deemed true and solid wisdom, consists almost entirely of two parts: the knowledge of God and of ourselves."
John Calvin

"The essence of Christian spirituality is following Christ on a journey of personal transformation that occurs only when God and self are both deeply known. Both, therefore, have an important place in Christian spirituality. There is no deep knowing of God without a deep knowing of self, and no deep knowing of self without a deep knowing of God... The distant land to which we are called in the new creature into which Christ wishes to fashion us – the whole and holy person that finds his or her uniqueness, identity, and calling in Christ."
David Benner

THE OLD + THE NEW

"I do not understand what I do. For what I want to do I do not do, but what I hate I do... For I know that good itself does not dwell in me, that is, in my sinful nature. For I have the desire to do what is good, but I cannot carry it out. For I do not do the good I want to do, but the evil I do not want to do – this I keep on doing."
Romans 7:15, 18-19

"...put off your old self, which is being corrupted by its deceitful desires; to be made new in the attitude of your minds."
Ephesians 4:22-23

"...and put on the new self, which is being renewed in knowledge in the image of its Creator."
Colossians 3:10

"...created to be like God In true righteousness and holiness"
Ephesians 4:24

"...and your life is now hidden with Christ in God"
Colossians 3:3

THE ENNEAGRAM
Greek : "Nine Drawing"

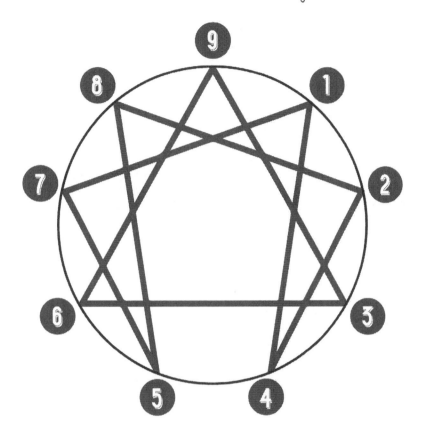

The Enneagram is an ancient tool that helps describe your personality in terms of who you are and how you relate to God, to others, and to yourself. It illustrates the nine archetypal human character structures; the nine beautifully flawed ways of being in the world. Combining ancient wisdom and modern psychology, this profoundly complex tool reveals nine unique sets of coping mechanisms that we've wrapped up around a childhood wound so that we don't have to face the pain It has caused us.

The Enneagram exposes the ways we have been uniquely wounded by sin and are motivated by guilt, fear, and shame, which severely handicap our capacity for trust and deep relationship. Better understanding our core motives, fears and sin strategies allows for tremendous spiritual growth and greater freedom from the unhealthy patterns that keep us stuck.

While at first glance it may seem restrictive or limiting, the Enneagram doesn't put you in a box. Rather, it turns the light on and reveals the box you're already in so you can finally get out. It maps the escape route and helps shed light on the hard and holy road back to wholeness.

Yes, friends, it is true: the truth will set you free, but first it might make you miserable. Embrace the discomfort. In order to grow more fully into the man or woman God created you to be, you must first shed your protective seed coating, and quite possibly, come undone.

> "For a seed to achieve it's greatest expression, it must come completely undone.
> The shell cracks, it's insides come out and everything changes.
> To someone who doesn't understand growth, it would look like complete destruction."
> Cynthia Occelli

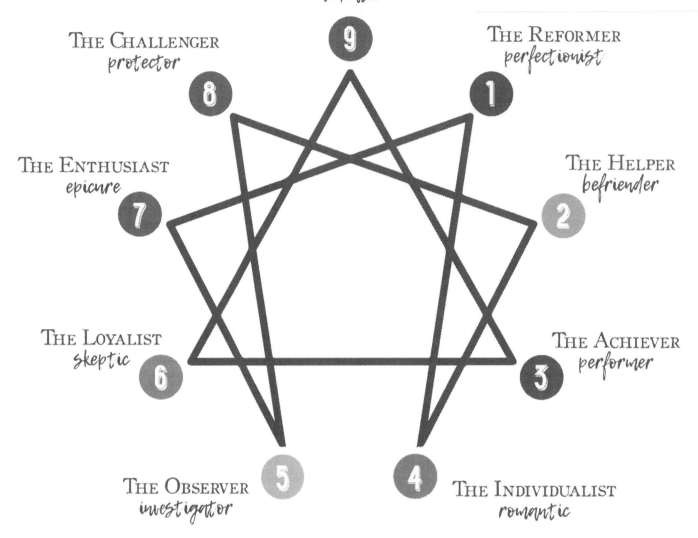

THE PEACEMAKER
mediator
9

THE CHALLENGER
protector
8

THE REFORMER
perfectionist
1

THE ENTHUSIAST
epicure
7

THE HELPER
befriender
2

THE LOYALIST
skeptic
6

THE ACHIEVER
performer
3

THE OBSERVER
investigator
5

THE INDIVIDUALIST
romantic
4

THE NINE TYPES IN A NUTSHELL

TYPE ONE is principled, purposeful, self-controlled, and perfectionistic.

TYPE TWO is generous, demonstrative, people-pleasing, and possessive.

TYPE THREE is adaptable, excelling, driven, and image-conscious.

TYPE FOUR is expressive, creative, empathetic, and temperamental.

TYPE FIVE is perceptive, innovative, secretive, and isolated.

TYPE SIX is engaging, responsible, anxious, and suspicious.

TYPE SEVEN is spontaneous, versatile, acquisitive, and scattered.

TYPE EIGHT is self-confident, decisive, willful, and confrontational.

TYPE NINE is receptive, reassuring, complacent, and resigned.

THE CENTERS | TRIADS

The Enneagram describes three '**centers of intelligence**' and perception: **heart, head and body**. While all of us have all three centers, our personality type has a dominant home base in one of the triads. Understanding our primary center gives us important insight into developing our personal and professional potential, and overcoming our blind spots, as well as assisting in identifying our dominant Enneagram type/number.

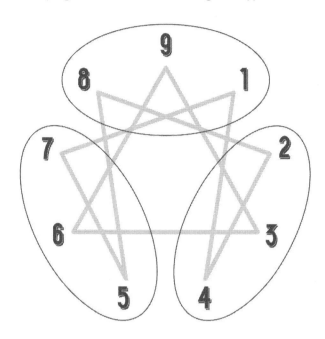

HEART | *The Feeling / Emotion Center*
Heart types emphasize the heart for positive and negative feelings, empathy, and concern for others, romance and devotion. Their focus is on success and relationship, performing up to expectations of the job or other people. They desire significance and identity, and they are shame driven.
"I am what others say or think about me"

2 : The Helper | 3 : The Achiever | 4 : The Individualist

HEAD | *The Thinking / Intellectual Center*
Head types lead with ideas, perception and rational thinking. They emphasize gathering information and figuring things out before acting. Their focus is on creating certainty and safety, or finding multiple options. They desire security and safety, and they are fear driven.
"I am what I have"

5 : The Observer | 6 : The Loyalist | 7 : The Enthusiast

BODY | *The Instinctual Center*
Body types lead with the body for movement, sensate awareness, gut-level feelings, personal security and social belonging. Their focus is on being in control of themselves and their environment, and taking action in practical ways. They desire control and justice, and are anger driven.
"I am what I do"

8 : The Challenger | 9 : The Peacemaker | 1 : The Reformer

TYPE & CENTER
Relationship with the Core Emotions
The Enneagram Institute | Don Riso + Russ Hudson

Each type results from a particular relationship with a cluster of issues that characterize their Intelligence Center. Most simply, these issues revolve around a powerful, largely unconscious emotional response to the loss of contact with the core of the self.

In the **Feeling/Emotion Center (HEART), the emotion is Shame**, and in the **Thinking/Intellectual Center (HEAD), it is Fear**. In the **Instinctive Center (BODY), the emotion is Anger or Rage.**

Of course, all nine types contain all three of these emotions, but in each Center, the personalities of the types are particularly affected by that Center's emotional theme. Thus, each type has a particular way of coping with the dominant emotion of its Center.

HEART | The Feeling Center

TWOS attempt to control their shame by getting other people to like them and to think of them as good people. They also want to convince themselves that they are good, loving people by focusing on their positive feelings for others while repressing their negative feelings (such as anger and resentment at not being appreciated enough). As long as Twos can get positive emotional responses from others, they feel wanted and are able to control feelings of shame.

THREES try to deny their shame, and are potentially the most out of touch with underlying feelings of inadequacy. Threes learn to cope with shame by trying to become what they believe a valuable, successful person is like. Thus, Threes learn to perform well, to be acceptable, even outstanding, and are often driven relentlessly in their pursuit of success as a way of staving off feelings of shame and fears of failure.

FOURS attempt to control their shame by focusing on how unique and special their particular talents, feelings, and personal characteristics are. Fours highlight their individuality and creativity as a way of dealing with their shameful feelings, although Fours are the type most likely to succumb to feelings of inadequacy. Fours also manage their shame by cultivating a rich, romantic fantasy life in which they do not have to deal with whatever in their life seems drab or uninteresting to them.

HEAD | The Thinking Center

FIVES have fear about the outer world and about their capacity to cope with it. Thus, they cope with their fear by withdrawing from the world. Fives become secretive, isolated loners who use their minds to penetrate into the nature of the world. Fives hope that eventually, as they understand reality on their own terms, they will be able to rejoin the world and participate in it, but they never feel they know enough to participate with total confidence. Instead, they involve themselves with increasingly complex inner worlds.

SIXES exhibit the most fear of all three types, largely experienced as anxiety, which causes them to be the most out of touch with their own sense of inner knowing and confidence. Unlike Fives, Sixes have trouble trusting their own minds, so they are constantly looking outside themselves for something to make them feel sure of themselves. They might turn to philosophies, beliefs, relationships, jobs, savings, authorities, or any combination of the above. But no matter how many security structures they create, Sixes still feel doubtful and anxious. They may even begin to doubt the very people and beliefs that they have turned to for reassurance. Sixes may also respond to their fear and anxiety by impulsively confronting it— defying their fear in the effort to be free of it.

SEVENS have fear about their inner world. There are feelings of pain, loss, deprivation, and general anxiety that Sevens would like to stay clear of as much as possible. To cope with these feelings, Sevens keep their minds occupied with exciting possibilities and options— as long as they have something stimulating to anticipate, Sevens feel that they can distract themselves from their fears. Sevens, in most cases, do not stop merely at thinking about these options, however. As much as possible they attempt to actually do as many of their options as they can. Thus, Sevens can be found staying on the go, pursuing one experience after another, and keeping themselves entertained and engaged with their many ideas and activities.

BODY | The Instinctual Center

EIGHTS act out their anger and instinctual energies. In other words, when Eights feel anger building in them, they immediately respond to it in some physical way, raising their voices, moving more forcefully. Others can clearly see that Eights are angry because they give themselves permission to express their anger physically.

NINES deny their anger and instinctual energies as if to say, "What anger? I am not a person who gets angry." Nines are the type most out of touch with their anger and instinctual energies, often feeling threatened by them. Of course, Nines get angry like everyone else, but try to stay out of their darker feelings by focusing on idealizations of their relationships and their world.

ONES attempt to control or repress their anger and instinctual energy. They feel that they must stay in control of themselves, especially of their instinctual impulses and angry feelings at all times. They would like to direct these energies according to the dictates of their highly developed inner critic (superego), the source of their strictures on themselves and others.

Notes + Doodles

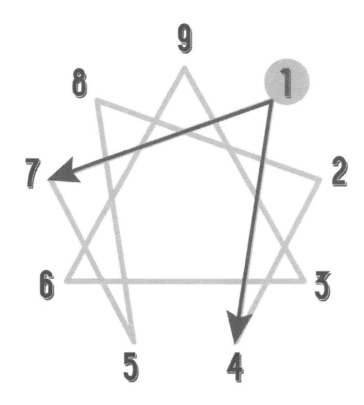

1 | THE REFORMER | PERFECTIONIST
Meticulous • Idealist • Principled • Critical

Ones are motivated by a need to perfect themselves, others, and the world, but sometimes that might mean they're too critical or perfectionistic. They see flaws and what's not right/fair with the world, follow rules, and act as the world's referees. Ones are highly principled, self-controlled and compulsively choose what is "right." Their core motivation is to be right and good.

In unhealth, Ones are rigid, judgmental and controlling. Under stress they are only able to subscribe to black and white thinking. In health, Ones have high integrity, are discerning, do excellent work and can accept the tensions (gray areas) of life. In relationship, Ones can sound critical even though their intentions are lovingly motivated.

DIVINE GIFT: **GOODNESS**

NEED: **TO BE PERFECT**

FOCUS: **WHAT'S WRONG?**

SEEK: **INTEGRITY**

ROOT SIN: **RESENTMENT/ANGER**

AVOIDS: **CRITICISM**

FEAR: **BEING CORRUPT/BAD**

GROWTH: **PATIENCE**

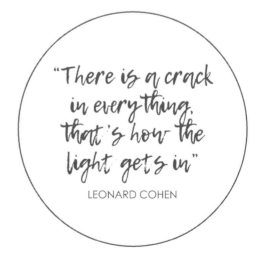

"There is a crack in every thing, that's how the light gets in"
LEONARD COHEN

SECURITY: 7 (spontaneous) | STRESS: 4 (moody)

9 WING: "The Idealist" | 2 WING: "The Advocate"

FAMOUS ONES

Biblical Characters:

the Apostle Paul, the older brother (in prodigal son story)

Historical Characters + Celebrities:

Harry Truman, Martha Stewart, Bill Maher, Hillary Clinton, Gandhi

Fictional Characters:

Atticus Finch (To Kill A Mockingbird), Randall Pearson (This Is Us), Hermione Granger (Harry Potter), Steve Rogers (Captain America), Peter Pevensie (The Chronicles of Narnia), Mary Poppins

SPIRITUAL GROWTH + FREEDOM

The lie believed: "It's not ok to make a mistake, I have to be perfect."

The truth received: "You are loved for who you are, not how good you are."

How to be Real: Pursue grace; Make allowance for my own & other's faults; Seek God and not perfection

How to love them well: Avoid power struggles. Admit when you are wrong. Don't flaunt your achievements. Bring novelty & fun to relating to help mitigate their worry.

The Good News for Ones:

The key verse that Ones must commit to memory is Romans 5:8, "God shows his love for us in that while we were still sinners, Christ died for us." This verse tells me that God knows all my sin and imperfections and still loves me. In Christ, I am truly known and fully loved. I am loved for who I am, not because of how good I am, but solely because of Jesus. Jesus was good in my place. All of my imperfections were put on Jesus, the Perfect One, who loved me and gave Himself up for me. He walked out of the grave to reform and perfect every part of creation and every part of me in due time. Through His Spirit I now have His righteousness credited to me. This means God doesn't see me and love me just as I am; even better, God sees me and loves me just as Jesus is—righteous.

Notes + Doodles

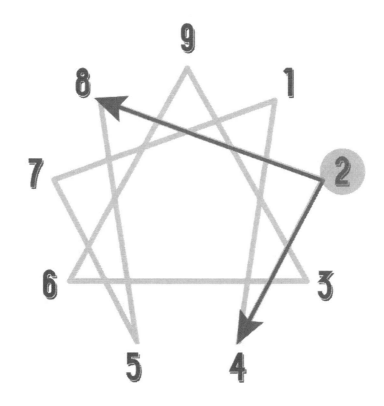

2 | THE HELPER | BEFRIENDER
Relational • Generous • Insecure • Demonstrative

Twos are friendly and warm, motivated by a need to be needed, so can also have problems with possessiveness and not acknowledging their own needs. They are generous and helpful companions. Their core motivation is to feel loved and connected.

In unhealth, they are prideful, people pleasing, score-keeping and manipulative to get what they want - the appearance of connection. In health, Twos have good boundaries, self-care and give selflessly without resentment. In relationship, Twos give generously but need to feel that you see their sacrifice and will reciprocate.

DIVINE GIFT: **LOVE**

NEED: **TO BE NEEDED**

FOCUS: **OTHER'S NEEDS**

SEEK: **CONNECTION**

ROOT SIN: **PRIDE**

AVOIDS: **OWN NEEDINESS**

FEAR: **BEING USELESS/UNLOVED**

GROWTH: **HUMILITY**

"Sometimes you don't realize you're drowning while trying to be everyone else's anchor"

SECURITY: 4 (self-caring) | STRESS: 8 (domineering)

1 WING: "The Servant" | 3 WING: "The Host/Hostess"

FAMOUS TWOS

Biblical Characters:

Martha, the Apostle John (the "beloved")

Historical Characters + Celebrities:

Mr. Rogers, Princess Diana, Desmond Tutu, Barbara Bush

Fictional Characters:

Michael Scott (*The Office*), Jack Pearson (*This Is Us*), Hagrid (*Harry Potter*), Dr. McCoy (*Star Trek*), Samwise Gamgee *(The Lord of the Rings)*, Peeta Mellark *(The Hunger Games)*, Dori (*Finding Nemo*)

SPIRITUAL GROWTH + FREEDOM

The lie believed: "It's not ok to be needy; I must meet needs."

The truth received: "You are loved simply for who you are, not because of what you do."

How to be Real: Watch how my pride affects the way I see myself and others; check my motives. Learn to confess my sin of pride. Be honest about my needs. Who I am comes from God's love, not from what I do.

How to love them well: Notice them and thank them for their service. Let them serve you, but don't abuse them. Have them name something you can do for them. Invite them over when you don't need something done.

The Good News for Twos:

The Scripture Twos should memorize is John 13:8. Jesus says to Peter, "Unless I wash you, you have no part in me." Twos are more comfortable doing the washing. Pride will cause them to want to resist being served by others. But Jesus solemnly warns Peter that if he doesn't humble himself and admit his weakness and neediness, then he cannot have a relationship with Jesus. For Jesus came to serve, not to be served. Twos must allow themselves to be served by Jesus and others, in order to experience the love they long for. Because Jesus's grace is sufficient, I am free to assume the posture of a child, admit my neediness, and walk in humility (2 Cor. 12:9). His grace is sufficient for me, so I don't have to feel shame related to my needs and weakness. And in Christ I have a High Priest who is able to sympathize with me, since Jesus became man (Heb. 4:15). In essence, Jesus became needy so that I can be needy with Him, without the feeling of shame. The incarnation and the cross tell me how much He wants me.

Notes + Doodles

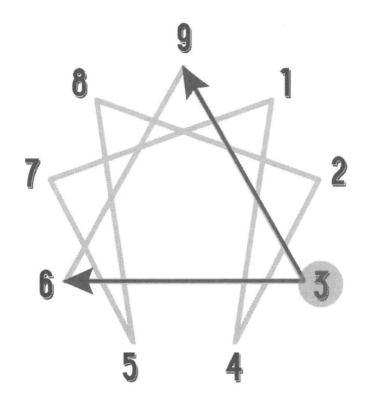

3 | THE ACHIEVER | PERFORMER
Image-Conscious • Ambitious • Adaptable • Motivated

Success-oriented, image-conscious and wired for productivity, Threes are motivated by a need to be (or appear) successful and to avoid failure. They are assertive and action-oriented. They get the job done. Their core motivation is to feel valued and to contribute. Underneath their achieving exterior lies a sensitive heart that cares what you think about them.

In unhealth, they are deceptive, competitive, unable to be vulnerable, and doggedly maintain a façade of success. In health, Threes are truly authentic, genuine and interdependent. In relationship, Threes fear you only want them for what they can do for you. They thrive on loyalty, encouragement and being valued for who they are over what they do.

DIVINE GIFT: **HOPE**

NEED: **TO SUCCEED**

FOCUS: **TASKS + GOALS**

SEEK: **VALUE**

ROOT SIN: **VANITY/DECEIT**

AVOIDS: **FAILURE**

FEAR: **BEING WORTHLESS**

GROWTH: **TRUTHFULNESS**

"For the first time I see the image of my brokenness utterly worthy of love"

SLEEPING AT LAST

SECURITY: 6 (trusting) | STRESS POINT: 9 (paralyzed)

2 WING: "The Charmer" | 4 WING: "The Professional"

FAMOUS THREES

Biblical Characters:

Jacob, Moses

Historical Characters + Celebrities:

George Washington, Tony Robbins, Oprah Winfrey, Prince William

Fictional Characters:

Andy Bernard (*The Office*), Tom Haverford (*Parks and Rec*), Draco Malfoy (*Harry Potter*), Scarlett O'Hara (*Gone with the Wind*), Boromir & Gimli (*The Lord of the Rings*), Don Draper (*Mad Men*)

SPIRITUAL GROWTH + FREEDOM

The lie believed: "It's not ok to be seen as a failure."

The truth received: "You are loved for who you are, not for what you accomplish or achieve."

How to be Real: Get honest with myself. Get more passionate about following Christ's Word, not dreams. Regularly confess my sins to others.

How to love them well: Encourage them to celebrate success; Be real with them; Accept that they are a little crazy; Encourage them to connect with their feelings; Thank them specifically.

The Good News for Threes:

The Scripture Threes should commit to memory is 1 Corinthians 13:1. Successes or failures don't matter. "What matters is whether or not the motive behind the behavior is love or self-exaltation." Without the core motivation of love, Paul says our efforts are but a noisy gong or clanging cymbal. In other words, we are only seeking to draw attention to ourselves and impress. When ambition and accomplishments are the ultimate goal, love is never present. Threes must remember the love of Christ that leads to humility and looking after the interests of others (Phil. 2:4). Jesus loved me and gave Himself for me, not my successful, accomplished, perfect image (Gal. 5:20). I am naked and exposed before Him (Heb. 4:12). He knows the real me—with all my sin and imperfections. The good news is that He has covered up my shame with His unconditional love and mercy (Rom. 5:8). I don't have to present myself as accomplished and put-together because Jesus is my true identity. Right now I am being transformed by the Holy Spirit into my true self, which bears the image of Jesus (2 Cor. 3:18).

Notes + Doodles

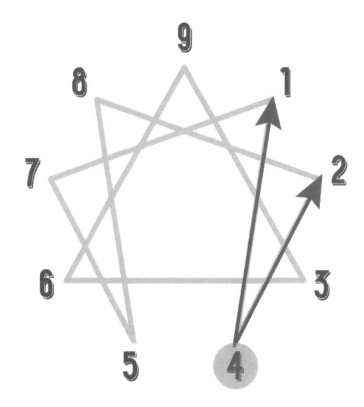

4 | THE INDIVIDUALIST | ROMANTIC
Dramatic • Artistic • Melancholic • Intuitive

Creative, sensitive and temperamental, Fours are motivated by a need to be special. They are emotionally honest but can also be moody and self-conscious. Fours are unique, emotionally deep, and into beauty. Their core motivation is to feel unique and significant.

In unhealth, Fours are dramatic, attention-seeking, temperamental, self-absorbed and labor under a nagging feeling that they are incomplete. In health, Fours see, know and understand themselves, thus satisfying their nagging hunger inside, in God. In relationship, respect and admire their individuality, understand they struggle under the weight of their own emotional world. Allow them to inspire our own uniqueness.

DIVINE GIFT: **DEPTH**

NEED: **TO BE SPECIAL**

FOCUS: **WHAT'S MISSING?**

SEEK: **IDENTITY**

ROOT SIN: **ENVY**

AVOIDS: **ORDINARINESS**

FEAR: **BEING UNNOTICED**

GROWTH: **CONTENTMENT**

"Those who were seen dancing were thought to be insane by those who could not hear the music"

NIETZSCHE

SECURITY: 1 (balanced) | STRESS: 2 (martyr-like)

3 WING: "The Aristocrat" | 5 WING: "The Bohemian"

FAMOUS FOURS

Biblical Characters:

King David

Historical Characters + Celebrities:

Michelangelo, Steve Jobs, Bob Dylan, Edgar Allan Poe

Fictional Characters:

Anne Shirley (Anne of Green Gables), Eeyore (Winnie the Pooh), Marianne Dashwood (Sense and Sensibility), Jay Gatsby (The Great Gatsby), Frodo Baggins (The Lord of the Rings), Loki (Thor)

SPIRITUAL GROWTH + FREEDOM

The lie believed: "It is not ok to be too functional or too happy."

The truth received: "You are seen and valued for who you are."

How to be Real: Listen to others when they share stories of suffering to realize it's not just you. Find and express appreciation for others' giftedness rather than focusing on what's missing. Look for beauty in the ordinary.

How to love them well: Don't put them in a box. Enjoy and appreciate how deeply they feel. Point out how their uniqueness has blessed you. Challenge them to feel, but not be led by their feelings. Enjoy the ride.

The Good News for Fours:

The Scripture Fours should commit to memory is John 15:11, "These things I have spoken to you, that my joy may be in you, and that your joy may be full." The "these things" that Jesus is referring to are unpacked in John 15:1-10, the essence of which is summed up when He says, "Abide in me, and I in you" (15:4). Jesus is describing the glorious reality of the mutual indwelling of God and man through faith in the gospel. This is uniquely meaningful for a Four in that it reassures them that nothing is missing. Their identity and sense of self is complete in Christ. Their joy is full, for it is the very joy of Jesus Himself. This reassures the Four that in the end melancholy will not win, for joy comes in the morning. Because of Jesus I can be unique or different without using my uniqueness as a way of measuring my self-worth. Jesus demonstrated a particular love for me when He gave His life for me on the cross (Gal. 5:20). What his love says about me is more than enough for me and completes my identity and joy. I don't have to live out the false narratives in my mind. Instead, I can live out the infinitely beautiful narrative of the gospel about the God who became man and lived, died, and was raised for me, so that I can know Him as Father and be part of His family. This is the greatest expression of truth, beauty, and goodness, which has become my own expression through the power and presence of the Holy Spirit.

Notes + Doodles

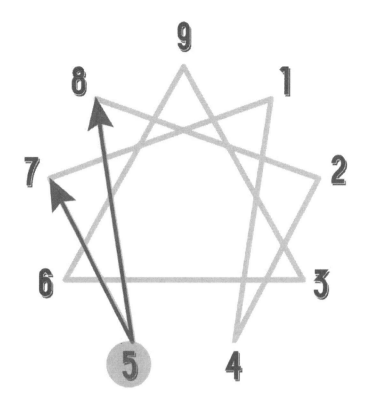

5 | THE OBSERVER | INVESTIGATOR
Perceptive • Detached • Informed • Introverted

Analytical, innovative and private, Fives are motivated by a need to gain knowledge, conserve energy, may be seen as intense, and avoid relying on others. They are natural experts, highly logical, critical thinkers, very objective and usually introverted. Their core motivation is to be capable, competent, self-sufficient and unique.

In unhealth, Fives become isolated, secretive, easily overwhelmed. In health, Fives are smart, curious, helpful and independent. In relationship, respect their lower energy level, they really serve the people they love the most. They can feel mysterious or invisible in a group. Respectfully utilize their expertise.

DIVINE GIFT: **WISDOM**

NEED: **TO BE PERCEPTIVE**

FOCUS: **WHAT MAKES SENSE?**

SEEK: **CLARITY**

ROOT SIN: **AVARICE/GREED**

AVOIDS: **FOOLISHNESS**

FEAR: **BEING DEPLETED/HELPLESS**

GROWTH: **GENEROSITY**

"Your mind is your instrument. Learn to be its master and not its slave"

SECURITY: 8 (assertive) | STRESS: 7 (impulsive)

4 WING: "The Iconoclast" | 6 WING: "The Problem Solver"

FAMOUS FIVES

Biblical Characters:

Luke, Thomas

Historical Characters + Celebrities:

Bill Gates, Friedrich Nietzsche, Jane Goodall, Albert Einstein

Fictional Characters:

Sherlock Holmes, Smaug (*The Hobbit*), Elrond (The Lord of the Rings), Dwight Schrute (*The Office*), Albus Dumbledore (*Harry Potter*), Gregory House (House), Sheldon Cooper (Big Bang Theory)

SPIRITUAL GROWTH + FREEDOM

The lie believed: "You are strong enough to not need the assistance and comfort of others."

The truth received: "Your needs are not a problem."

How to be Real: Get out of my head and get in touch with my feelings. Wisdom doesn't come from being alone (Proverbs 18:1). Lean into conversations, community and relationships. Information does not equal transformation (knowledge of the Bible doesn't lead to salvation, a relationship with Jesus does).

How to love them well: Acknowledge their need for personal space and time. Express what it means to you when they engage. Don't criticize how they have fun. Utilize their knowledge and wisdom.

The Good News for Fives:

The Scripture Fives should commit to memory is Deuteronomy 6:5, "Love the Lord your God with all your heart and with all your soul and with all your strength". This verse reminds us that human beings are made to worship God with their whole selves and not just the mind. Engaging the emotions and the body is necessary for ongoing transformation for Fives. Because of Jesus I do not have to protect myself from intrusion and letting myself be known. The gospel tells me that Jesus has broken into my world and invaded me (Luke 2:8-14; Acts 9:1-19). This is good news because it means that Jesus knows the real me and He loves the real me (Gal. 2:20). I no longer have to live a compartmentalized life of strategic self-protection. The Spirit of God has given me the only knowledge I need to feel safe—a saving knowledge of the truth (1 Tim. 2:4).

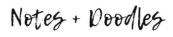

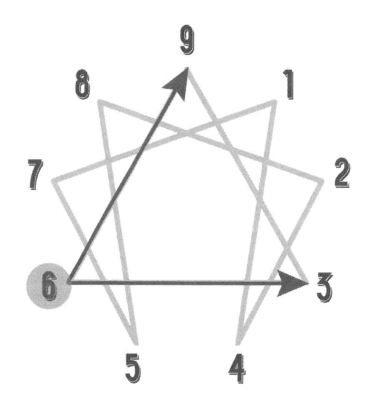

6 | THE LOYALIST | SKEPTIC
Fearful • Committed • Procrastination • Loyal

Sixes are dutiful, reliable and practical, and are motivated by fear and the need for security. They are responsible, committed, loyal and fearful. Their core motivation is to be supported, safe and secure.

In unhealth, Sixes are highly anxious, faithless, overly reliant on "experts" and masters of the worst-case-scenario. In health, Sixes become grounded in themselves and their own inner authority, trusting in God's goodness in the mystery of life. In relationship, Sixes are fiercely loyal, highly dependable, in it for the long haul and have good senses of humor.

DIVINE GIFT: **FAITHFULNESS**

NEED: **TO BE SECURE**

FOCUS: **DANGER/WORST CASE**

SEEK: **GUIDANCE**

ROOT SIN: **ANXIETY/FEAR**

AVOIDS: **DEVIANCE**

FEAR: **BEING DEFENSELESS**

GROWTH: **COURAGE**

SECURITY: 9 (serene) | STRESS: 3 (frenetic)
5 WING: "The Defender" | 7 WING: "The Buddy"

"I choose to believe I was made to be a sanctuary"

SLEEPING AT LAST

18

FAMOUS SIXES

Biblical Characters:

Ruth, Apostle Peter

Historical Characters + Celebrities:

Richard Nixon, George Bush, Malcolm X, Ellen DeGeneres

Fictional Characters:

Thorin Oakenshield (*The Hobbit*), Spiderman, Narcissa Malfoy
(*Harry Potter*), Marilla Cuthbert (Anne of Green Gables), Cowardly Lion (*The Wizard of Oz*), George
Costanza (Seinfeld), Mulan

SPIRITUAL GROWTH + FREEDOM

The lie believed: "It is not okay to trust yourself."

The truth received: "You are safe."

How to be Real: Be strong and courageous and do the work. God alone is my refuge. Focus on the truest truth and bravely follow God.

How to love them well: Be secure and consistent; always tell the truth. Thank them for their loyalty to you. Encourage them to be courageous. Fiercely support them when they are right. Lovingly correct them when they are being paranoid.

The Good News for Sixes:

The Scripture Sixes should commit to memory is 1 Peter 5:6-7, "Humble yourselves, therefore, under God's mighty hand, that he may lift you up in due time. 7 Cast all your anxiety on him because he cares for you." Sixes will have their fear transformed into courage and confidence as they humble themselves before God and cast their anxieties on Him. The most important thing for Sixes to remember is that they are safe to come to God with their fears because "He cares for them." Sixes can rest and act courageously because they have a God who promises to take care of them. When they doubt this truth, they need only to look at the cross to see the extent of God's loving care. Sixes should regularly call to memory the truth of 1 John 4:18, that "perfect love casts out fear." God has stewarded His authority to love and not harm. God's love is ultimately safety, for it is our salvation. Jesus subjected Himself to the anxieties and dangers of this world and of sin, death, and the devil so that I can be safe. Ultimately, "fear has to do with punishment," and Jesus has taken my punishment and saved me from God's wrath (1 John 4:18). By faith, Jesus dwells in my heart and I dwell in Him (Eph. 3:17). We are safe at home in one another (John 14:20). I am fully hidden in Christ, my refuge, my rock (Col. 3:3).

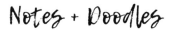

Notes + Doodles

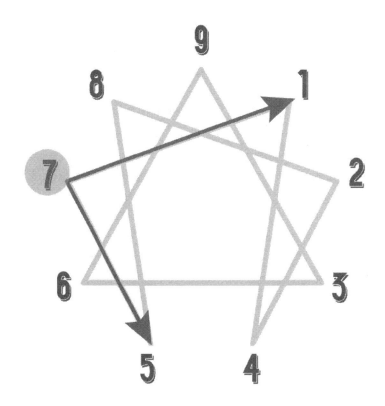

7 | THE ENTHUSIAST | EPICURE
Entertaining • Accomplished • Uninhibited • Spontaneous

Sevens are fun, spontaneous and adventurous, and are motivated by a need to be happy, to plan stimulating experiences, and to avoid difficult feelings, which can lead to impatience and impulsivity. They are entertaining, versatile and scattered. Their core motivation is to be satisfied and fulfilled.

In unhealth, Sevens are pain avoidant, impulsive and fearful of being trapped. In health, Sevens learn to savor and are naturally filled with gratitude. In relationship, Sevens can be flighty, they need new challenges or help staying the course.

DIVINE GIFT: **JOY**

NEED: **TO AVOID PAIN**

FOCUS: **WHAT'S NEXT?**

SEEK: **FREEDOM**

ROOT SIN: **GLUTTONY**

AVOIDS: **PAIN/SUFFERING**

FEAR: **BEING TRAPPED**

GROWTH: **SOBER JOY**

SECURITY: 5 (grounded) | STRESS: 1 (complaining)
6 WING: "The Entertainer" | 8 WING: "The Realist"

"Let's climb this mountain before we cross that bridge"

SLEEPING AT LAST

FAMOUS SEVENS

Biblical Characters:

King Solomon, Barnabas

Historical Characters + Celebrities:

Robin Williams, Thomas Jefferson, John F. Kennedy, Thomas Edison

Fictional Characters:

Iron Man, Phoebe Buffay (Friends), Sirius Black (Harry Potter), Peregrin Took (The Lord of the Rings), Kevin Pearson (This Is Us), Lydia Bennet (Pride and Prejudice), Peter Pan

SPIRITUAL GROWTH + FREEDOM

The lie believed: "It is not okay to depend on anyone for anything."
The truth received: "You will be taken care of."

How to be Real: Practice contentment by learning to reflect and thank God for what He has done. Embrace pain (the depth of my pain is directly proportional to the height of my joy). Commit to friendships through the tough times.

How to love them well: Give them lots of room to play. Recognize when they choose to deal with problems. Acknowledge how much joy they bring to your life, and join in the fun.

The Good News for Sevens:

The Scripture Sevens should commit to memory is John 15:11, "These things I have spoken to you, that my joy may be in you, and that your joy may be full." The "these things" that Jesus is referring to are unpacked in John 15:1-10, the essence of which is summed up when He says, "Abide in me, and I in you" (15:4). Jesus is describing the glorious reality of the mutual indwelling of God and man through faith in the gospel. This is uniquely meaningful for a Seven in that it reassures them that no experience or substance can give them the joy they're longing for. Their identity and sense of self is complete in Christ. Their joy is Jesus' joy. This is the essence of the abundant life Sevens long for (John 10:10). The world is so broken that Jesus had to come and die to restore it. This means I don't have to paint my life in beautiful colors. The cross frees me to be honest about the painful parts of my story and about my own brokenness. I am so bad Jesus had to die for me to save me. It is also true that I am so loved that Jesus was glad to die for me! It was for the joy set before Him that He endured the cross (Heb. 12:1). I do not have to try to fill the void in my life or cover up my pain because in spite of my brokenness Jesus loves me and gave Himself for me.

Notes + Doodles

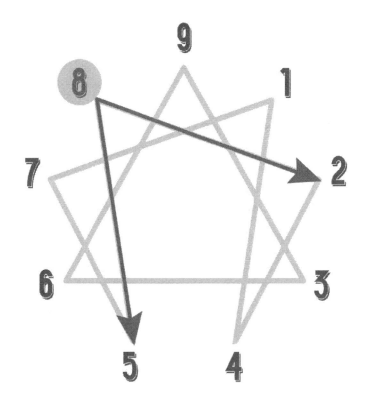

8 | THE CHALLENGER | PROTECTOR
Self-Confident • Decisive • Just • Leader

Commanding, intense and confrontational, Eights are motivated by a need to be strong and to assert control over the environment and others to avoid revealing weakness or vulnerability. They are natural born leaders. Their core motivation is to be strong and in control of themselves.

In unhealth, Eights are dominating, controlling and aggressive. In health, Eights use their strength in service of others, advocate for justice and are awesome leaders. In relationship, Eights can feel brash or controlling. Adjust to being refreshed by bald-faced honesty for a change and don't shrink away. Don't be "mean" to them, just interact with their ideas and bring your own.

DIVINE GIFT: **POWER**

NEED: **TO BE AGAINST**

FOCUS: **TAKING CHARGE**

SEEK: **POWER**

ROOT SIN: **LUST**

AVOIDS: **VULNERABILITY**

FEAR: **BEING CONTROLLED**

GROWTH: **TENDERNESS**

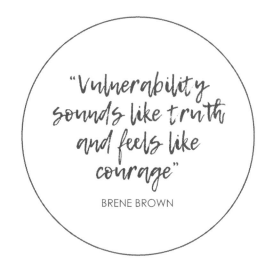

"Vulnerability sounds like truth and feels like courage"

BRENE BROWN

SECURITY: 2 (altruistic) | STRESS: 5 (withdrawn)

7 WING: "The Maverick" | 9 WING: "The Bear"

FAMOUS EIGHTS

Biblical Characters:

John the Baptist, Miriam, Samson

Historical Characters + Celebrities:

Muhammad Ali, MLK Jr., Mother Teresa, Napoleon Bonapart

Fictional Characters:

Jack Bauer (24), Alastor Moody (Harry Potter), Rhett Butler (Gone with the Wind), Beth Pearson (This Is Us), Jeanine Matthews (Divergent), Inspector Javert (Les Misérables), Mr. Incredible

SPIRITUAL GROWTH + FREEDOM

The lie believed: "It is not okay to be weak, you cannot trust anyone."

The truth received: "You do not have to be strong to be loved."

How to be Real: Learn to show mercy toward others. Learn to be willing to yield to others. Find someone I am willing to be vulnerable with. When I am weak, I am strong; my weakness leads me to depend on God.

How to love them well: Notice when they are tender, compassionate or sweet. Speak directly to them; don't shower them with flattery. Stand up for yourself, but also stand up with them when they are right. Don't assume they mean to be hurtful.

The Good News for Eights:

The Scripture Eights should commit to memory is 2 Corinthians 12:9, "But he said to me, "My grace is sufficient for you, for my power is made perfect in weakness." Therefore I will boast all the more gladly about my weaknesses, so that Christ's power may rest on me." In this passage Paul admits that he is weak. Rather than defending himself through an image of power, Paul owns his weakness, which, he says, keeps him humble and dependent upon the grace and power of God. "Therefore," Paul says, "I will boast all the more gladly of my weaknesses, so that the power of Christ may rest upon me" (12:9). I do not have to be strong and in control because Jesus is my strength, and He is in control. When I was weak and helpless, He used His perfect power to come to my aid and rescue me from my sin and false self. He has proven trustworthy and that His love for me is unconditional. This means I am free to be vulnerable with God and others and boast all the more of my weaknesses without fear of being dominated or controlled, for I am controlled with the love of Christ (2 Cor. 5:14).

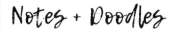

Notes + Doodles

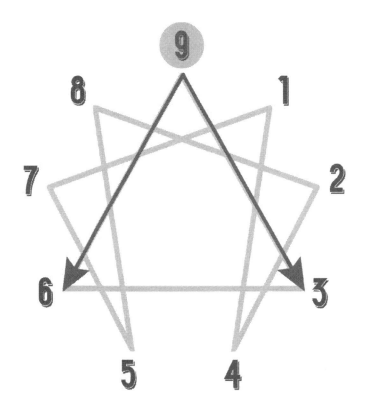

9 | THE PEACEMAKER | MEDIATOR
Peaceful • Reassuring • Complacent • Neglectful

People who are dominant in this type are easygoing and value unity. They are accepting and supportive, but that can lead to them becoming too complacent. Nines are "easy"; open, comforting, self-denying. Their core motivation is simple: peace.

In health, Nines discover their voices and live out of a secure sense of self. They use their peacemaking abilities to bring harmony to groups. In unhealth, Nines are passive-aggressive, highly avoidant of problems and negligent of themselves. In relationship, they merge with others, so seek their opinions and give them time to process and respond.

DIVINE GIFT: **PEACE**

NEED: **TO AVOID**

FOCUS: **AGENDA OF OTHERS**

SEEK: **HARMONY**

ROOT SIN: **SLOTH**

AVOIDS: **CONFLICT**

FEAR: **BEING INSIGNIFICANT**

GROWTH: **ENGAGEMENT**

"Wake up and say yes to the adventure that is your life"

SECURITY: 3 (focused) | STRESS: 6 (doubtful)

8 WING: "The Referee" | 1 WING: "The Dreamer"

FAMOUS NINES

Biblical Characters:

Jonah

Historical Characters + Celebrities:

Abraham Lincoln, Dalai Lama, Gerald Ford, Tony Bennett

Fictional Characters:

Harry Potter, Kate Pearson (This Is Us), Dorothy (The Wizard of Oz), Jane Bennet (Pride and Prejudice), Winnie the Pooh, Jerry Gergich (Parks and Rec), Jim Halpert (The Office), Sleeping Beauty

SPIRITUAL GROWTH + FREEDOM

The lie believed: "It is not okay to be bold and assert yourself."

The truth received: "Your presence and opinion matter."

How to be Real: Own and resolve my own feelings. Embrace healthy conflict, and that it can actually lead to resolution and harmony. Make declarative statements about my wants and needs as a means for deeper connection with others. Pursue faith with action (cultivate a practice-based faith, rather than just a beliefs-based faith).

How to love them well: Create an environment where their voice is heard and it matters. Don't shield them from all conflict; encourage them to actively engage because conflict brings growth. Celebrate with them when they finish projects. Don't push them to sprint, let them find their rhythm. Thank them for their gift to see the other side of things.

The Good News for Nines:

The Scripture Nines should commit to memory is Ephesians 4:15: "Rather, speaking the truth in love, we are to grow up in every way into Him who is the head, into Christ." The temptation for Nines is to withdraw and check out. Therefore, they must learn to trust their intuition, assert their presence, and exercise their voice. This is what Paul is exhorting us to do in this verse. The body of Christ will not grow into the fullness of Christ apart from the boldness to speak the truth in love. Nines are good with the "in love" part. It's lacking the courage and clarity to speak the truth that they struggle with. The world needs their objectivity and voice, for they have unique ability to harmonize and restore peace. So in faith they must learn to be bold and declare the truth in love. They can replace their fear of conflict with comforting reality that declaring the truth is the loving thing to do. My ultimate peace is found in Christ, not my circumstances. I have been justified by faith and have peace with God through my Lord Jesus Christ (Rom. 5:1). Jesus has solved my deepest conflict with God and has made me God's dear child. He has quieted my soul's deepest struggle with guilt by becoming my sin and my righteousness. I don't have to fear being good enough because I have Jesus, and He is my peace that surpasses all understanding (Phil. 4:7). He is the God of peace who is always with me (Phil. 4:9). I can rest because in Christ I am known and loved by God.

Notes + Doodles

SUBTYPES | Instinctual Variants

The instinctual subtypes of the Enneagram are the **self-preservation, one-to-one** (also referred to as sexual) and **social** instincts. The insight of this specific component boils down to an individual's hierarchy of emotional needs. All of us have all three needs (social, one-to-one/sexual and self-preservation), but our experiences and wiring cause us to need/desire/cling to one more than the others. The beauty of subtypes is that it further broadens the 'flavor' of each Enneagram type by revealing 27 instinct-based "sub-personalities"; more nuanced versions of the main type (each type goes to an even more granular level when factoring in the instinct *sequence* of our subtype stacks: dominant, auxiliary and repressed).

SELF-PRESERVATION | **Values safety, provision and comfort above all else, the need/focus is to survive through reserving, gaining or needing resources.**

People of the self-preservation variant are generally trying to be comfortable and independent. Their well-being is very important to them, so they pay much attention to their health, house and financial position. They are less interested in interpersonal contact, and are typically less spontaneous and don't show as much emotion as people of the other two subtypes of their enneagram type.

ONE-TO-ONE / SEXUAL | **Values intensity of experience and chemistry (attraction/draw), the need/focus is deep intimacy above all else.**

People of the sexual variant are very much interested in one-to-one connection. They are looking for intimacy and this may show in sexuality, though not necessarily. Being in a relationship is very important to them. They are the most passionate of the subtypes, being temperamental and having more energy. They have less of a problem with getting into a fight and care less about rules and responsibility.

SOCIAL | **Values social hierarchy and the way they fit into its structure. The need/focus is to contribute to society and be known in a communal way.**

People of the social variant prefer to be in groups or teams. They are more interested than the other subtypes in the position that they and others have in a group, and are consequently concerned with status. Wanting to be accepted, they try to fit in and be nice.

THE **27** SUBTYPE PERSONALITIES

The Complete Enneagram: 27 Paths to Greater Self-Awareness

by Beatrice Chestnut

TYPE ONE

Self-Preservation Ones focus on making everything they do more perfect. They are the true perfectionists of the Enneagram. They see themselves as highly flawed and try to improve themselves and make every detail of what they do right. These people are the most anxious and worried Ones, but also the most friendly and warm.

Social Ones focus on doing things perfectly in a larger sense—knowing the right way to do things—and modeling how to do things right for others. An intellectual type, these Ones have a teacher mentality; they see their role as helping others see what they already know–how to be perfect.

One-to-One Ones focus on making other people—and society as a whole—more perfect. More reformers than perfectionists, they tend to display more anger and zeal than the other Ones. These Ones focus less attention on perfecting their own behavior and pay more attention to whether or not others are doing things right.

TYPE TWO

Self-Preservation Twos seek to gain approval through being charming and youthful. Less oriented to giving and more burdened by helping, they charm others into liking them as an unconscious effort to get people to take care of them. More self-indulgent, playful, and irresponsible than the other two Twos, they are more fearful and ambivalent about connecting with others.

Social Twos seek to gain approval from others through being powerful, competent, and influential. More a powerful, leader type of person, they take charge of things and play to a larger audience as a way of proving their value.

One-to-One Twos gain approval through being generous and attractive. They emphasize their personal appeal and promises of support to make others like them and do things for them—this is a more emotional, passionate Two who seduces specific individuals.

TYPE THREE

Self-Preservation Threes work hard to assure material security for themselves and the people around them. Oriented to being good (as well as looking good) according to social consensus, they want to appear successful, but they don't want to brag or self-promote in an obvious way (because that wouldn't be good). SP Threes are self-sufficient, extremely hard-working, results-oriented, and modest.

Social Threes work hard to look flawless in the eyes of others. Oriented to competing to win and attaining the material and status symbols of success, they focus on getting things done and always having the right image for every social context. The most aggressive, competitive, well-known Three, Social Threes enjoy being onstage and know how to climb the social ladder.

One-to-One Threes focus on creating an image that is appealing to others and supporting and pleasing the people around them—especially partners, co-workers, and family members. They have a relationship or team mentality and work very hard to support the success of others (rather than their own).

TYPE FOUR

Self-Preservation Fours are stoic, strong, and long-suffering—emotionally sensitive on the inside, they often don't communicate their darker feelings to others. While they feel things deeply, and may feel sad inside, they often have a sunny, upbeat exterior, as they often received the message early on that their caretakers couldn't handle their pain or darker emotions. They may feel anxious inside, but they tough things out and have a high tolerance for frustration.

Social Fours suffer. They focus on their own emotions and the underlying emotional tone of whatever situation they are in. They compare themselves to others and tend to see themselves as less worthy or lacking in some way. They are more emotionally sensitive than most other types, they wear their feelings on their sleeve, and connect to themselves through the authenticity of their emotional truth.

One-to-One Fours are more assertive and competitive. These Fours are not afraid to ask for what they need or complain when they don't get it. They can appear aggressive to others, and they strive to be the best.

TYPE FIVE

Self-Preservation Fives focus mainly on maintaining good boundaries with others. Friendly and warm, SP Fives like to have a private space they can withdraw to if they want to be alone. They focus on minimizing needs, finding refuge, and having all they need within their place of safety.

Social Fives enjoy becoming experts in the specific subject areas that interest them. They like acquiring knowledge and connecting with others with common intellectual interests and causes. They may be more connected to people they connect with through a social cause or are of expertise than the people in close proximity in everyday life.

One-to-One Fives have more a stronger need to connect with other individuals–under the right conditions.

These Fives are more in touch with their emotions inside, though they may not show it on the outside. They have a romantic streak that they may express through some form of artistic expression.

TYPE SIX

Self-Preservation Sixes are the more actively fearful (the phobic or "flight") Six. They doubt and question things in an effort to find a sense of certainty and safety (that often eludes them). They seek to be warm and friendly to attract allies as a form of outside support or protection in a dangerous world.

Social Sixes are more intellectual types who find a sense of safety in following the guidelines of a system or way of thinking to feel protected by a kind of impersonal outside authority. They tend to be logical, rational, and concerned with reference points and benchmarks. They are more sure of things than the SP Six, who expresses more doubt and ambiguity, and can even become "true believers."

One-to-One Sixes cope with underlying fear (that they may not be aware of) by appearing strong and intimidating to others. Of the "fight" or "flight" reactions to fear, they choose "fight," and tend to be risk-takers, contrarians, or rebels. They have an inner program that tells them that the best defense is a good offense.

TYPE SEVEN

Self-Preservation Sevens are very practical. Good at getting what they want, they readily recognize opportunities and know how to make things happen, whether through pragmatic planning or a network of allies. They tend to have a talkative, amiable, hedonistic style.

Social Sevens want to avoid being seen as excessively opportunistic and self-interested, so they focus on sacrificing their immediate desires to pursue an ideal of being of service to others. They take responsibility for the group or family and want to be seen as good by easing others' suffering.

One-to-One Sevens are idealistic dreamers, who have a need to imagine something better than what might be true in their everyday reality. Extremely enthusiastic and optimistic, they have a passion for seeing things as they could be or as they imagine them to be (as opposed to how they really are).

TYPE EIGHT

Self-Preservation Eights focus on getting what they need to survive in a direct, no-nonsense way. They have a low tolerance for frustration and a strong desire for the timely satisfaction of their material needs. They know how to do business and get things done and don't need to talk about it very much.

Social Eights focus on protecting and mentoring others they are connected to or anyone they view as needing their support. While they can be rebellious and assertive, they appear less aggressive as they have a softer side when it comes to taking care of others.

One-to-One Eights have a strong rebellious tendency and like to be the center of things. More provocative and passionate than the other Eights, they like to have power over people and situations.

TYPE NINE

Self-Preservation Nines focus on finding comfort in familiar routines and the satisfaction of their physical needs. Whether through eating, sleeping, reading, or doing crossword puzzles, SP Nines tend to lose themselves in whatever activities help them feel grounded and comfortable.

Social Nines focus on working hard to support the groups they are a part of as a way of seeking a sense of comfort in belonging. Congenial people who like to feel a part of things, Social Nines tend to be light-hearted and fun, and expend a lot of effort in doing what it takes to be admitted to and supportive of the group or community.

One-to-One Nines tend to merge with the agenda and attitudes of important others in their lives. Sweet, gentle, and less assertive than other types, this relationship-oriented Nine may take on the feelings and opinions of the people they are close to without realizing it.

HORNEVIAN GROUPS
Stance Triads

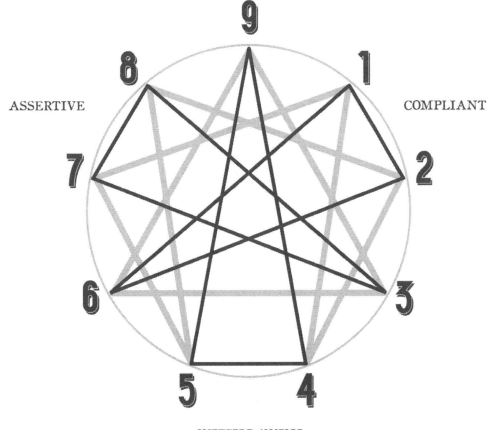

WITHDRAWING STANCES | FOURS, FIVES, NINES

This triad is seen as moving *away* from others, focusing on thinking and feeling, making them highly imaginative. These people are slow to act because they are often more shy or introverted. Their orientation to time is the *past*.

COMPLIANT STANCES | ONES, TWOS, SIXES

This triad moves with or *toward* others, focusing on feeling what is happening around them and then acting accordingly. These people are very concerned with others' expectations. Their orientation to time is the *present*.

ASSERTIVE STANCES | THREES, SEVENS, EIGHTS

This triad is seen as standing independently and, at times, as moving *against* others. These people are happy to be in charge of others, and they put their agendas first. Their orientation to time is the *future*.

BUILDING A MORE CHRIST-LIKE
+ Compassionate Community

The better we can understand the way we've been wired or are bent, the easier it is to recognize patterns and tendencies, and course correct when necessary. This knowledge also profoundly impacts the way in which we relate to the world around us.

AWARENESS OF THE UNIQUE AND BRILLIANT WAYS IN WHICH WE HAVE BEEN WIRED BY OUR CREATOR HELPS CULTIVATE EMPATHY AND COMPASSION.

"All of you together are Christ's body, and each of you is a part of it."
1 Corinthians 12:27

TOGETHER WE MAKE UP THE BODY OF CHRIST; A BODY COMPRISED OF INCREDIBLY DIFFERENT, ASTONISHINGLY DIVERSE, UNIQUELY CALLED AND EQUIPPED HUMAN BEINGS — SLOWLY BEING RESTORED TO THEIR ORIGINAL GLORY.

THE MORE SELF-AWARE WE BECOME, THE HEALTHIER WE WILL BECOME, AND THE HEALTHIER AND MORE EFFECTIVE THE COLLECTIVE BODY OF CHRIST WILL BECOME.

"Self-knowledge is tied with inner work, which is both demanding and painful. Change occurs amid birth pangs. It takes courage to walk such a path. Many avoid the path of self-knowledge because they are afraid of being swallowed up in their own abysses. But Christians have confidence that Christ has lived through all the abysses of human life and that he goes with us when we dare to engage in such confrontation with ourselves."
Andreas Ebert

"God's image has been imprinted uniquely on each of us.
In God's infinite creativity there are no duplicates;
you are the only you there has ever been or ever will be."
Dick Staub

"In light of all this, here's what I want you to do...get out there and walk - better yet, run! - on the road God called you to travel. I don't want any of you sitting around on your hands. I don't want anyone strolling off, down some path that goes nowhere. And mark that you do this with humility and discipline—not in fits and starts, but steadily, pouring yourselves out for each other in acts of love, alert at noticing differences and quick at mending fences."
Ephesians 4:1-3 (MSG)

ENNEAGRAM RESOURCES

This workshop + companion guide has taken shape around what I've gleaned through these excellent books, teachings and interviews. I trust they will be a great source of information, insight and encouragement as you continue on your own Enneagram journey.

BOOKS
• **The Road Back to You** by *Ian Cron + Suzanne Stabile*
• **Self to Lose, Self to Find** by *Marilyn Vancil*
• **Mirror for The Soul** by *Alice Fryling*
• **The Gift of Being Yourself** by *David G. Benner*
• **The Essential Enneagram** by *David Daniels*
• **The Sacred Enneagram** by *Christopher Heuertz*
• **The Enneagram** | A Christian Perspective by *Richard Rohr*
• **The Path Between Us** by *Suzanne Stabile*
• **The Enneagram and the Way of Jesus** by *AJ Sherrill*
• **Personality Types + The Wisdom of the Enneagram** by *Hudson + Riso*
• **The Complete Enneagram**: 27 Paths to Greater Self Knowledge by *Beatrice Chestnut*

TESTS
www.wepss.com | $10
www.enneagraminstitute.com/rheti | $12
www.integrative9.com/GetYourType | $23+
www.exploreyourtype.com/details | FREE
www.yourenneagramcoach.com/p/dont-know-your-type | FREE
*Remember that the best way to accurately discover your dominant type is to spend some time with the 9 type descriptions (motivations, tendencies, fears, etc.) – you'll know when it's you!

PODCASTS + MUSIC
• **The Road Back to You** Podcast with *Ian Cron + Suzanne Stabile*
• **Typology Podcast** with *Ian Cron*
• **The Enneagram Journey Podcast** with *Suzanne Stabile*
• **Sleeping At Last** (musician, *Ryan O'Neal*) is writing + recording a song for each of the 9 numbers
www.sleepingatlast.com
*Beth McCord and Christopher Heuertz have both done excellent interviews on different shows on the subject of the enneagram – simply search for their names to find the episodes.

COACHING + DISCIPLESHIP
• Coaching + Online Training with Beth McCord www.yourenneagramcoach.com
• Spiritual Formation Plan for each of the 9 types from Fellowship Paragould:
www.fellowshipparagould.com/resources#resources-2
• 'YOU' Sermon Series by Matt Brown, Sandals Church : www.sandalschurch.com/watch/a-series-called-you

"You cannot help but learn more as you take the world into your hands. Take it up reverently, for it is an old piece of clay, with millions of thumbprints on it."

John Updike

FIND YOUR TYPE

1 | The Reformer

- o Do you continually think about ways you could have done something better or ways you might have responded to a person or a situation more to your advantage?
- o Is there a voice in your mind that criticizes everything you do and many things other people do?
- o Have you frequently had to sacrifice your desires or opportunities because people close to you are more verbal or more aggressive about their needs, or because they have needs that seem to take priority?
- o Do you make "To Do" lists for yourself and for others?
- o When you are working on a project, do interruptions break your concentration on the details and trigger a "slow burn" of anger?
- o Do you think you try hard at everything in life and often wish you could be more laid back or easygoing?
- o Do you feel revulsion toward people who are always needy or looking for a "free ride" in life and silently criticize them for not taking charge of their own lives?
- o When planning to make a purchase, do you ignore the person who tries to give you a sales pitch and look for someone who will give you the information you need and let you make up your own mind?
- o Do you consistently find yourself redoing tasks because others failed to do them right the first time?

- • "I must strive to meet high standards of behavior and performance to avoid criticism and feelings of failure."
- • "Pretty much everything in the world can be improved, and some parts definitely should be"
- • "Perfect is hard. It should be hard. It's rare and it's hard. But it's worth it."
- • "If everyone did their part to follow what they know are the rules of decent society, everything would flow much more smoothly."

2 | The Helper

- o Are you so sensitive and responsive to the pain in people around you that others might good-naturedly refer to you as a "mind reader" or "psychic"? Do you find it difficult to limit the time or energy you spend when others seem to need you?
- o Do you struggle with organization in your personal life -- starting many projects but following through on very few?
- o Is it difficult for you to judge how much time is appropriate for yourself or others to focus on meeting personal needs without becoming selfish?
- o Are you a flexible, accepting person who seldom, if ever, finds strictly right or wrong answers to life's problems?
- o In personal relationships, does your dedication to finding creative ways of expressing your affection often collide with feelings of resentment over being taken for granted?
- o Do you quickly become agitated or "stressed out" when doing tasks that focus on theoretical, objective issues that are devoid of any interpersonal dimension?
- o No matter where you are -- on the job, shopping, on vacation, at a restaurant, at a party -- do you seem to attract people, even perfect strangers, who pour out their hearts or tell you their life stories?
- o Do you gain a sense of personal fulfillment at helping others achieve their goals?

- • "If I express my real feelings, desires and needs (the core attributes of my real, unlovable self), I will be rejected or humiliated."
- • "Not having many needs myself, it's easier to sacrifice my own needs in the service of meeting other people's needs (and making them happy) than to assert any needs or desires."
- • "Conflict produces bad feelings and disapproval and risks damaging relationships, so it should be avoided."
- • "Most people don't like needy people who cause trouble or create conflict by expressing negativity, strong feelings or opinions."

3 | The Achiever

- o Do you sometimes think you're too cynical or suspicious because you intuitively seem to know the hidden motives of others -- especially their dark, manipulative intentions?
- o Are you able to be positive, optimistic, and upbeat around others even though you feel pessimistic or desperate about your life when you're alone?
- o Do you guard against becoming too emotionally vulnerable or dependent upon even those closest to you because you fear being manipulated?
- o When your goals are unclear or you don't have any goals, do you lose your energy and find that life is suddenly dull and boring?
- o To avoid being rude or hurtful, do you often have to feign interest in a conversation you're having because a new idea or important current project is beginning to race through your mind?
- o Do you prize relationships that are free and undemanding and break relationships that become too complicated or time consuming?
- o Are you able instantly to hide your feelings of shock, disappointment, anger, embarrassment, and so on until you can deal with them in private?
- o Would you tend to err on the side of saying too little rather than saying too much?
- o Is it difficult for you to take time for yourself, to relax or to "do nothing" when there are still projects left undone?

- • "People admire and respect success and achievement. To inspire admiration in others you must be successful and achieve."
- • "If you achieve high status, you are a valuable person in the eyes of society."
- • "Reaching specific goals depends upon hard work. I work hard to do whatever it takes to reach my goals and remove any obstacles in the way."
- • "It is important to have the right image for every context so that people will think well of you."

4 | The Individualist

- o Would you say that being with people, nurturing personal relationships, and being intensely loyal to the people you love are the innate gifts that bring the greatest pleasure and meaning to your life?
- o Even in your closest relationships, does fear of loss or abandonment cause you to struggle against feelings of jealousy or possessiveness?
- o Do you tend to avoid or procrastinate over tasks that require focusing on details or paperwork, seeing them as tedious and depressing?
- o When presented with a new plan, idea, or project, do you feel that it's important to recognize flaws first so that the possibilities won't become unrealistic and therefore disappointing?
- o Is your sense of meaning and purpose in life best expressed through the symbols, stories, and traditions that connect you to people, to your faith, or to life in general?
- o Have you spent a great deal of time and energy on a quest to understand the meaning of your own life and history, hoping to understand your purpose for being on this earth?
- o When experiencing the beauty of nature -- for example, a sunset or a budding flower -- do you connect with something spiritual and even sometimes feel your heart will burst because of the sheer wonder of creation?
- o Do you often feel so many emotions at once that you become confused about which to express first and how to organize your thoughts?
- o Are you attracted to the dramatic or unusual things in life -- in clothes, food, friends, art, decor?

- • "I am lacking some essential qualities of goodness, and so I will inevitably be rejected and abandoned by others."
- • "What I want eludes me, and what I can have seems somehow boring or lacking something essential. What is here and how is mundane and boring; what I desire most is ideal and at a distance."
- • "I lack some basic attributes that would allow others to really love me. But if I could find the ideal person who realizes how special I am, then maybe I could really experience what I long for."
- • "I'm special, but others don't recognize it. No one understands me. I am destined to be misunderstood. I feel as if I don't belong."

5 | The Observer

- o Do you relish and even require extended periods of time alone to ponder and sort out the important issues of life?
- o Do you have an unquenchable thirst for new experiences, new adventures, or new knowledge, and are you quickly bored by repetition?
- o Do you usually have a point of view different from everyone else's and find yourself amazed at the lack of rational thinking behind others' conclusions?
- o Do you enjoy talking about and planning a project for months, even years, but find your enthusiasm slipping away at the prospect of beginning the hard work of actually doing it?
- o In personal relationships, do you often feel frustrated and pull back because others misread your intentions?
- o Are you generally impatient with group decisions, becoming restless and irritated as others ramble on and on about unrelated, unimportant issues?
- o Do you tend to see the absurdity of life and enjoy throwing people off guard by pointing out the ridiculous with wit and humor?
- o Are the social interactions of your life initiated primarily by others, even when you want to be included or want some form of communication?

- • "People can be intrusive and threatening to my personal comfort. I must protect my time and energy by having firm boundaries and maintaining my private space; otherwise, others will deplete me."
- • "Overall, withdrawing/separation from others feels more comfortable than the alternative."
- • "It's better and safer to feel my emotions when I am by myself (and not when I am in the presence of others) so the safest course of action is to withdraw."
- • "Knowledge is power, and is best obtained through observation, research and the collection and comparison of data."

6 | The Loyalist

- o As you get up in the morning, are you enlivened when you have a full schedule of diverse activities for the day?
- o Are you generally more at ease entertaining in the comfort of your own surroundings, even though it means more work for you?
- o Would you say that dedication to home, family, marriage, and/or community are the basic values out of which you live your life?
- o As a person who takes responsibility seriously, do you often resent and feel overburdened by the number of people who make irresponsibility a way of life?
- o As a general rule, do you need to gather the opinions of others -- family, friends, co-workers -- before making a decision?
- o Having strong opinions about life, do you mistrust and become upset with people who attempt to justify and expand the "gray areas"?
- o Do you feel more connected with people who are important to you when you know the details of what's going on in their lives on a regular basis?
- o Are you a hard-working, organized person who prefers to keep to a tight schedule, even to the point of scheduling your vacation or relaxation time?
- o Would you have more confidence in and loyalty toward an authority figure who laid down specific rules rather than one who was flexible and able to "go with the flow"?

- • "By imagining the worst thing that could happen, you can prepare for it and thus potentially protect yourself or ward it off in advance."
- • "By expecting and anticipating what might go wrong, you can guard against making mistakes, getting hurt or becoming trapped in a bad situation."
- • "Searching for certainty and gathering information in an uncertain world is one way to feel safer."
- • "It's good to be on guard about how people might threaten you, hurt you or take advantage of you, so you won't be taken by surprise and unable to protect yourself."

7 | The Enthusiast

- o When a situation becomes intense, do you get a nearly uncontrollable urge to laugh or to point out the absurdity of it all, often with a good one-liner?
- o When you hear about or see problems in the world or in people's lives, do you almost automatically start thinking of solutions?
- o Are you "turned off" when people tell you how gifted you are or what great potential you have because you know that underneath is the expectation for you to be doing something more meaningful or productive with your life?
- o Are you stimulated by intellectual sparring, by new and different experiences, or by the possibility of being on the cutting edge of a new venture but "turned off" at the thought of your life being stable, secure, and routine?
- o Do you prize flexibility and avoid making long-term commitments or plans "set in concrete"?
- o Do people almost universally enjoy your company but at the same time give you the feeling they don't see the deeper, more intelligent, more loyal side of your personality?
- o Do you see yourself as a good communicator with a broad enough range of interests that you can keep a conversation going with just about anyone?
- o Are you the kind of person who, if given the opportunity, can see the potential use of many things others might throw out as junk?
- o Do you enjoy mental challenges and find yourself seeking out these kinds of challenges to keep life enjoyable or to keep from being bored?

- • "Life is about sampling as many good and fun things as possible."
- • "I must avoid experiencing pain, discomfort or boredom, because if I allow myself to experience these emotions, I will likely become stuck in them for a long time, perhaps even forever."
- • "Limitations of any kind lead to negative feelings, and they should be avoided."
- • "Why would anyone want to dwell in discomfort if they could be happy instead? Being happy and staying upbeat is a sensible, reasonable, worthy goal."

8 | The Challenger

- o Do you have clear and firm ideas about what is right and wrong in situations that are important to you?
- o Do you generally find that you need to be alert for people with hidden agendas?
- o Do you find that the most irritating and difficult people to deal with are those who beat around the bush and never directly say what is on their minds?
- o Would you agree that indecision is the greatest thief of opportunity and therefore a valid argument against getting caught in group decision making?
- o Are you at ease in leadership positions and find them falling naturally into your lap?
- o Do you find that others often simply expect or assume that you will take charge?
- o Do you think of yourself as a practical person who understands what it takes to get the job done?
- o Are you the kind of person who is unafraid to take a stand against injustice, especially injustice toward people who are unable to defend themselves?
- o Do you generally express your views just as intensely as you feel them and even feel exhilarated in a discussion in which everyone disagrees?

- • "In a tough world, you need to be tough to survive. It's bad to be weak or vulnerable. Weak people are not worthy of respect."
- • "Other people do not have the power to limit me in what I want and what I do. I have the power to make things happen and do what I want."
- • "Powerful people tend to take advantage of weaker individuals. I protect the people I care about."
- • "While I don't necessarily "like" conflict, I can confront others when I need to move forward, get what I want, protect someone or combat injustice."

- Are you known as an easygoing, affable, common-sense kind of person even when inside you may be feeling very different?

- Is there a place in your home that you find comfortable and relaxing and to which you generally gravitate to think, read, or relax?

- Do arguments make you so uncomfortable that you avoid them, even to the point of walking out of the room when they begin?

- Are you greatly attracted to outdoor activities, and do you find being in nature an almost sacred experience of freedom?

- Do you feel that the best way to prevent trouble is to keep your thoughts to yourself and let the other person do the talking, even if you don't agree?

- Do you see yourself as an independent person who can do what you need or want to do and not be swayed by group pressure?

- Would you agree that in general people create most of their own difficulties because they take life too seriously and get all worked up over very minor things?

- Do you enjoy thinking your way through puzzling questions, and do you often find practical answers to intricate problems?

- When given the option, would you avoid sophisticated political or social gatherings, choosing instead the quieter, simpler pleasures of life?

- "I don't matter. It's easier that way. What I think and feel isn't that important. And that's okay. Other people just feel more strongly about things than I do."

- "It's not okay to be angry or upset because that puts you at odds with others. It's more important to be nice and peaceful than to be true to myself."

- "I don't know what I want, and it's not important anyway."

- "Knowing what I want and asserting my desires in the world of others takes too much work and will alienate people I need or want to stay connected to. It's easier to go along with what other people want than to go to the trouble of asserting what I want."

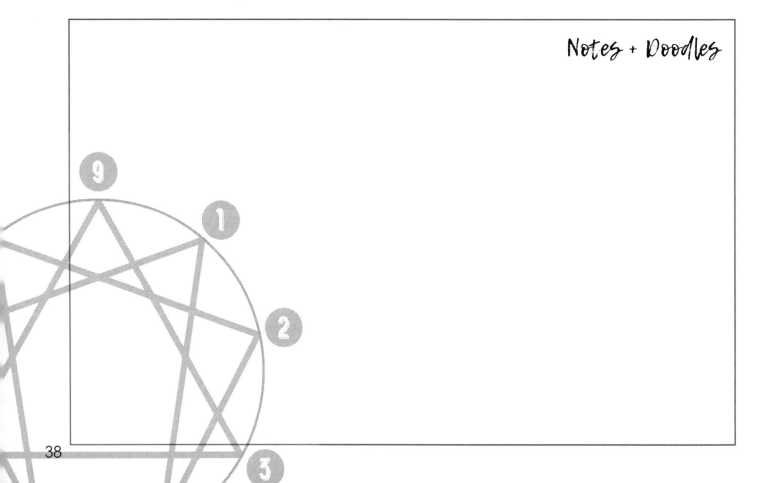

Notes + Doodles

For Longing

BY JOHN O'DONOHUE

IRISH PRIEST

BLESSED BE THE LONGING THAT BROUGHT YOU HERE

AND QUICKENS YOUR SOUL WITH WONDER.

MAY YOU HAVE THE COURAGE TO LISTEN TO THE VOICE OF DESIRE

THAT DISTURBS YOU WHEN YOU HAVE SETTLED FOR SOMETHING SAFE.

MAY YOU HAVE THE WISDOM TO ENTER GENEROUSLY INTO YOUR OWN UNEASE

TO DISCOVER THE NEW DIRECTION YOUR LONGING WANTS YOU TO TAKE.

MAY THE FORMS OF YOUR BELONGING — IN LOVE, CREATIVITY, AND FRIENDSHIP —

BE EQUAL TO THE GRANDEUR AND THE CALL OF YOUR SOUL.

MAY THE ONE YOU LONG FOR LONG FOR YOU.

MAY YOUR DREAMS GRADUALLY REVEAL THE DESTINATION OF YOUR DESIRE.

MAY A SECRET PROVIDENCE GUIDE YOUR THOUGHT AND NURTURE YOUR FEELING.

MAY YOUR MIND INHABIT YOUR LIFE WITH THE SURENESS

WITH WHICH YOUR BODY INHABITS THE WORLD.

MAY YOUR HEART NEVER BE HAUNTED BY GHOST-STRUCTURES OF OLD DAMAGE.

MAY YOU COME TO ACCEPT YOUR LONGING AS DIVINE URGENCY.

MAY YOU KNOW THE URGENCY WITH WHICH GOD LONGS FOR YOU.

Made in the USA
Columbia, SC
07 March 2020

88803292R00024